ANXIETY-FREE ME BOOK SERIES

Anxiety & Panic
WORKBOOK

Stop Stressing, Start Living

Best Selling Author of
You 1 Anxiety o

JODI AMAN

Ja'Love Books

Ja'Love Books

919 S Winton Rd.
Rochester NY 14618

This book is available at quantity discounts for educational use. For further information, please contact info@jodiaman.com

This publication is designed to provide practical recommendations to ease anxiety suffering. It is not meant to replace the medical or mental health advice of your current provider. If further assistance is required, the services of a local competent professional should be sought.

Library of Congress Cataloging-in-Publication Data has been applied for.
Anxiety and Panic Workbook : stop stressing, start living / Jodi Aman
pages cm
ISBN: 978-0-9985613-5-6 (paperback)

Cover and interior design by Michelle Radomski of One Voice Can.

Introduction

Dearest Anxiety-Sufferers and Freedom Seekers,

- Do you feel out of control of your life?

- Are you feeling plagued by self-doubt? Do you worry that you can't handle difficult situations?

- Are you afraid of what people think or how they might judge you?

- Do you wish you had more confidence at work or in relationships?

- Has anxiety stopped you from doing things in your life that you would enjoy (or used to enjoy)?

Anxiety is one of the most horrible feelings in the world. I wouldn't wish it on my worst enemy. Unfortunately, so many people suffer from it at some time in their life. Even though it is highly treatable (I consider it fully curable), most people wait months or years before getting help.

However long you've waited, your suffering is about to end. You have this book in your hands.

First of all, you are not alone. I know first-hand how horrible anxiety feels. That's why I want to help you. I have been where you are. I had anxiety for two decades before I totally rid myself of it.[1] In the last 20 years, as a psychotherapist, I helped thousands of

---

1 My Anxiety Story: jodiaman.com/anxiety-story

people recover from anxiety with the skills that I learned to free myself. And now I want to share them with you.

My clients say that it helps them so much that I understand what they are going through. I know anxiety in a way that other therapists don't. I get them. I get you.

That is why I put together *Anxiety & Panic Workbook*. I hope to give you the tools you need to stand up to anxiety and get yourself free from it. But first, I want you to know that you can get better, even if you've had it for 20 years like I did.

The National Institute of Mental Health has shown that anxiety is the number one mental health problem in America. There are several reasons that make anxiety a pandemic in our culture.

1. Increase of virtual trauma.

2. Stress-evoking, inflammatory diet.

3. Fast paced society, with higher and higher social standards that we measure ourselves against.

These phenomena make us feel out of control and butcher our confidence. If you are curious about these, I explain them in detail in my bestselling book *You 1, Anxiety 0: Win your life back from fear and panic.*

Once you experience anxiety, it feels so bad, that it is understandable why you, I and most of the population get stuck there. I explain the how and why from the biological perspective in this video: jodiaman.com/biology-video.

I address natural ways to decrease anxiety, including diet, in my book: *Natural Ways to Solve Anxiety and Depression (releasing in late 2018).* Having physical reasons causing anxiety, doesn't mean that you can't get rid of it psychologically. I've seen it happen. I think of it as walking in a river against the current. You can still walk (resolve anxiety psychologically), it takes just a bit more effort. *Natural Ways to Solve Anxiety (and Depression)* is one tool to change the direction of the river.

However, no matter how we get anxiety, we can train our brains not to stay stuck there. This *Anxiety & Panic Workbook* is the tool that has you walking forward to happiness no matter what the current is. In it, I share 50 practical exercises that will have you learn about yourself, build trust and confidence, break anxiety down and get you to commit to going forth without it troubling you any longer.

How to use this book:

There are many ways to use this workbook. You can either do it in order, taking on an exercise or an activity every one or two days, or merely scroll through, pick something and try it. You will relate, like and receive more from some exercises than others. That's why I gave you so many.

If you find an exercise that you don't think would help you too much, try it anyway. Sometimes you don't know what kind of a-ha you will get until you are done. In fact, it may even come days later. I assure you that none of these exercises will hurt you. This is just practice. Once your favorites are discovered, you can repeat them over and over again in your own journal.

I still practice my most transformational exercises every day.

Remember that even when you feel good, you continue to generate happiness by taking care of yourself, by making and keeping commitments, by journaling, moving, engaging in something creative and by practicing good problem solving/decision making.

Let's get you started!

Motivation and Removing Barriers

First things, first, I want to know...

1. Are you ready to STOP feeling like this? _____

Why?

_____

_____

_____

It's time for you to live your life and be happy without the struggles and suffering from anxiety and panic!

Tell me what you would do if you didn't have anxiety?

_____

_____

_____

_____

_____

Do you wonder why your motivation is part of an anxiety workbook? _____

I don't want you to take your motivation for granted. It is your source of strength and energy for the practices I am about to show you. It'll give you the tenacity to stand up to the bully that anxiety has become in your life.

In fact, the success of your full recovery stands on how motivated you are to overcome it. I know that you want to get better. But are you actually willing to *do anything?*

I had a conversation with a woman recently who was telling me that her daughter was unwilling to go to counseling to help her with anxiety. She observed, "If I felt that bad, I would do anything to make myself feel better."

This stuck in my mind, and I kept thinking about it for the next few weeks. This mother suffered horribly with anxiety. As a friend of hers for many years, I have watched her dismiss all the things we both knew would help her feel better. Stop eating sugar. Do these stretches. Set limits with bullies. Go to this kind of doctor instead of that kind. Reach out when you need help.

"I know they will make me feel better, but I know myself, I just won't do that." She said about each one.

A woman in my last Anxiety Coaching Group[2] was in a terrible state of mind: full panic all day. She desperately asked what to do. I gave her small safe steps that would gain momentum and really help her calm herself. The next week she showed up on the call in the same state, having had no relief. She admitted not doing my suggestions and asked me again what she ought to do.

A family member of mine has anxiety. Whenever I invite him out, both of us knowing he's always better with people than home alone, he declines saying he is so anxious that *he can't.*

"Won't" and "can't" are ideas, not truths. If you believed it was absolutely *impossible* to get over anxiety, how much energy would you put into it? Absolutely none. Why waste time on impossibility?

Do you say that you are "willing to do anything," yet still have can't and wont's stop you?

---

2 jodiaman.com/group

These beliefs are insidious. You sometimes don't even know they are there, but they affect you mind, body and spirit.

Anxiety makes you think that you are protecting yourself with can'ts and won'ts, not to be disappointed if it doesn't work.

This is hogwash. The risk of disappointing yourself exponentially increases when you don't allow yourself to try.

If you are here, you must believe that it is possible, even if it is just remotely. Before we really get started, I want you to put power behind that possibility, and really believe it so anxiety can no longer convince you that the can'ts and won'ts are real.

Suspend all doubts for a moment. Doubts aren't protecting you. They have you suffering intensely in the present (staying anxious) so you can avoid an unconfirmed possibility of suffering in the future (being disappointed).

To heal, the first step is to believe it is possible. People who believe it is possible always get over their anxiety fast. They don't stay anxious for years.

Let's break down your doubts and make you a believer so there are no more barriers to your healing.

2. **Tell me where you are starting.** On a sale of 1–10, how sure are you that you can get over anxiety and live free from it?

_____

Anxiety throws a lot of so-called evidence to you about why you can't. Don't let this just lurk in your mind. Get it out in the open so we can dissect and debunk it.

Write why you think/feel that you can't: _____

_____

_____

_____

About any of the above that happened in the past: That was then, this is now. There is one thing I know: You have changed and learned and grown. What happened in the past is not evidence for what can happen in the future. Go back to the list above and cross out anything that happened in the past. What's left?

Now, write down FIVE reasons why you think it may be possible. (For example: 1. *Other people have cured themselves. 2. I had it before and then I was better for many years.*)

1. _____

2. _____

3. _____

4. _____

5. _____

Now, 1–10, how sure are you that you can do this? _____

Finding Motivation

Maybe merely "getting over anxiety" is not enough of a motivation. You must have something really precious that you NEED to hold onto no matter what. There was a woman who wanted to push past her fear of driving on the highway. She used to avoid it altogether taking regular streets everywhere. Week after week in therapy, we talked about things in her life that were bothering her and we kept postponing the work on her driving on a highway.

One day she said, "I must be putting that off because I am too scared."

I disagreed. She didn't have motivation for overcoming that fear since she worked around it in a mildly inconvenient way. The other subjects of our conversations were much more important to work through.

I asked her, "If one of your sons was in the hospital and the quickest way to get to him was on a highway, would you do it?"

She said, "Absolutely!"

I smiled. "The problem is not your fear; it is your lack of motivation."

When you live with anxiety for a long time, you work around it. These become familiar and comfortable, which makes it seem easier than pushing yourself to release it. You need motivation.

Check your motivation.

3. List ten examples of what you might do because it is so important to you, despite anxiety trying to stop you.

1. _____

2. _____

3. _____

4. _____

5. _____

6. _____

7. _____

8. _____

9. _____

10. _____

On a scale of 1-10, how motivated are you now to push past anxiety?

_____ Did it change? _____

Contemplate what you'll discover as you move past anxiety.

- Loving and connecting with people can enrich your life.

- Taking risks is more exciting than avoiding great opportunities.

- Reaching out is more satisfying than letting heartfelt words go unspoken.

- "Protecting" usually equals suffering.

- Living free beats living in fear any day of the week.

- Control is a matter of perception.

- Peace is available to anyone, even someone living in oppression.

Make a list now of the many cool things you can do when you're not restricted by anxiety. This is a list of optional things that are not important enough to do when you deal with anxiety. If you didn't have anxiety, however, they would be fun and totally worth it. In fact, they will make life more enjoyable.

If anxiety didn't stop me, I would...

_____

_____

_____

_____

_____

You may be still worried or convinced that it will be (too) hard. No. The work is actually easy. Anxiety wants you to think that it is hard. It wants you to think that you can't, so that you don't try. It wants to stay with you and continue to shut your life down.

This workbook will show you easy and absolutely safe practices. They may suggest steps outside your comfort zone, but you are here because your comfort zone is too small a circle and you are suffering inside there anyway. Also, you are literally safe way beyond your comfort zone. Feeling scared doesn't mean dangerous. I will not lead you into danger. In fact, we will leave your useful protective skills intact and make them even stronger in this process. You will not be vulnerable. You may feel it, but it won't be the slightest bit true.

You will be safe in this process. Anxiety will try to convince you that you are not safe, but you are absolutely, positively safe.

4. Begin with the end in mind.

Kinetic Affirmation with Visual Imagery

Close your eyes and conjure a scene of yourself in the future. You are doing something (i.e., cleaning your house, hiking in a park, out at a restaurant, running an errand, or attending a lecture) and you feel anxiety-free. You are happy and even smile at the relief of it. Take a deep breath and try to feel your body calm, cool and collected as you sit or stand relaxed and contently observing the world around you.

You can start this practice with a less stress-inducing activity and graduate to a more stress-full activity. Don't worry! You are just imagining it, not doing it yet.

---

3 This doesn't apply if you're CURRENTLY dealing with someone (personally or politically) who abuses you. Many parts of this book would read differently if I was advising someone in your situation. I am working on a book specifically for you, but it is not ready yet. For now, if you are looking for personal support, you can get some help from me here: jodiaman.com/counseling or with a local practitioner.

Getting to Know Anxiety in a New Way

5. Describe your anxiety:

_____

_____

_____

_____

_____

Anxiety wants you to think of it as SCARY, hard, powerful, horrible, and overwhelming. The reason is that this description gives it power, and it wants that power to stay.

It is important to know EVERYTHING about anxiety and see it from every perspective. When you know its power source, you can cut it off.

Why Anxiety Gets out of Hand

Lots of things happen to us in our life and they set off emotional responses. This is human. For example, you might feel "Loss" if someone breaks up with you. (See the black circle in Figure 1 that represents the amount of sorrow you feel.)

This is devastating enough. But it doesn't stop there. Next, you compound it by negatively judging your response. Am I overreacting? Why can't I keep a relationship?

How could I mess this up? Why does everyone leave me? (The dotted circles in Figure 1 represent the amount of unhappiness you feel from each of these thoughts.)

And then, fear sets in when you start worrying about how you can't handle feeling this bad over any amount of time. It happens mainly if you see yourself as someone with "no skills." How am I going to do this? How long is this going to last? I can't do this! OMG! OMG! I'm losing my mind! (The striped circles in Figure 1 represent the amount of worry you feel from each of these fears.)

Figure 1.

Black: Original feeling: "Loss"

Grey dotted: Negative self-judgments

Striped: Fears and anxieties

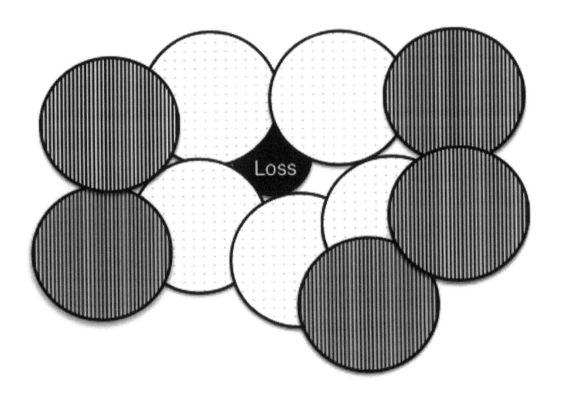

Note that the combination of the dotted and striped circles is bigger than the size of the black circle. The intensity of emotions has gone from the original small sorrow of loss "A" to the size of the entire misery of Figure 2 "B" with the negative self-judgments and fear. (See Figure 2.)

Figure 2.

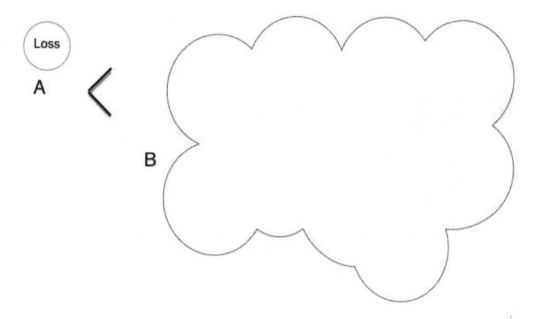

Usually you don't realize each of these separate steps. It feels like a single reaction and it's overwhelming. You often end up negatively judging yourself again on top of it all, adding insult to injury: Why do I take things so personally? Why am I not over this by now? My ex doesn't seem to be this upset. I'm so weak. The overwhelm-feeling expands. (Black dotted circles in Figure 3.)

Figure 3.

Black dotted: Secondary layer of negative self-judgments

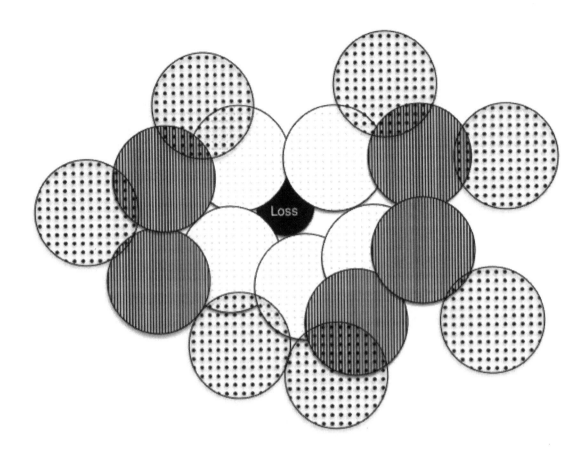

What does anxiety really mean?

Many words are used to describe anxiety. Everyone thinks of it and understands it differently. Whatever words you use to illustrate your anxiety come from your own experience, so go with it. Since I can't ask you what those words are, the following list explains how I'll use certain words in this workbook.

There may be terms here that you've never associated with anxiety. You'll find it helpful to see examples of how anxiety hides as other feelings and problems. Exposing these disguises will give you the advantage.

The **fear response** is the sympathetic nervous system response to dangerous or perceived dangerous stimuli where adrenaline is released into your blood stream causing increase in heart-rate, breathing and heat to prepare your muscles to fight or run, a hyper focused mind, tunnel vision, and an interrupted digestion in favor of sending blood to large muscles. All of these have a purpose to protect you if you were in danger. If or when you are safe (and you know that you are safe), the parasympathetic nervous system releases GABA to stop the adrenaline and calm you down.

Fear, as a noun, is a general term for this emotion and used to categorize other things or concepts you are afraid of. I.e., "I have a fear of public speaking." It is also used when speaking generally about the feelings of fear.

Worry is a thought or perception that something is cause for alarm or an anticipation that something bad will happen. You might worry about the bad that might happen, if you can't handle a situation. You might worry about other people's suffering or that something bad will happen to them.

Nervousness is usually described as a slight to moderate physical sensation with or without fearful thoughts. You may still be "handling it" at this point, but you're starting to worry and feel a bit out of your comfort zone. You may be able to push it aside, but you still fear that the worst is yet to come. With nervousness, you may avoid or opt out of plans or make adjustments to prevent your feelings from intensifying and miss out on experiences you'd otherwise enjoy.

Anxiety is a worry-based physically and emotionally intense sensation due to the release of cortisol and adrenaline hormones triggered by the fear response. It is the physical and emotional suffering that happens when you are not in physical danger but think and feel as though you are. It's usually accompanied by distressing thoughts as well as desperation to feel calm again because of the way adrenaline hyper focuses your mind. You feel helpless or worried that you "can't handle it" or that you'll "go crazy." You feel stuck, trapped in a feeling of vulnerability and out of control, even though you're not in immediate danger.

Panic is an amplification of anxiety that includes increased physical sensations and a feeling that you're in imminent danger. (If you were in danger, you'd use that energy to survive. When you're not in danger, it feels overwhelming.) You feel like you want to jump out of your skin, have a need to move your body by pacing or rocking because the adrenaline released gives you a boost of energy. You feel a sense of desperation for help, any help.

Uncomfortable is a word that many people use to describe their symptoms when they can't relate to the words above. They can relate to feeling uncomfortable even though they don't know why. Any discomfort that a person can't describe usually signifies nervousness.

Desperation is a mark of anxiety. It's the urgent desire to be anywhere other than where you are. Desperation confuses you into thinking that anxiety's demands are the ones you need to listen to in order to end your suffering. Such as urgently leave a situation, avoid something, and flee— but this often makes the situation worse in the long run.

Feeling **out-of-control** triggers anxiety. "Control issues" are anxiety issues. People who have control issues have them because they're afraid something bad might happen if they aren't overseeing and managing things. Being "out-of-control" feels vulnerable and this freaks us out.

Anger comes when something important to you is lost or threatened. It might also mean you are impatient to escape a feeling that's beyond uncomfortable. It is also expressed (or used as a power tactic to restore control) when you feel desperate or powerless. It is extremely common for anxiety to be behind anger.

Stress is like the fear response. It is an overall feeling of exhaustion caused by a pressuring or intense context. Physiologically, it's synonymous with fear, anxiety, and nervousness, because it's caused by the same release of hormones. Stress is socially acceptable, so it's a handy way to describe unwanted feelings without stigma.

Dread convinces you that a bad event is practically inevitable. You might expect that "the other shoe will drop." It's a tactic of anxiety and used by the mind to convince you to be vigilant when the dreaded thing happens.

OCD is where a person has obsessive thoughts that cause such intense anxiety that he or she engages in compulsive actions to try relieving that anxiety.

Embarrassment is used to describe the worry of what others think. This is often a component in social anxiety. People with social anxiety feel like everyone is looking at them and judging them. You have feelings of inadequacy, incompetency, insufficiency or deficit with embarrassment.

Shyness is instigated by worries. These worries can be varied. For example feeling inferior, worrying about being egotistical, worrying that people will misunderstand or judge you or your opinions as not worthy or wrong. You feel timid or concerned that you might hurt someone or that someone may hurt you.

Phobia is an intense fear of an object or situation that poses little actual danger except in some contexts, but provokes anxiety.

Social anxiety is very common. It's anxiety in social situations usually characterized by worrying about how things will go, how you come across to people, being judged by others and whether or not you'll feel comfortable in public or with a group.

"Lazy" is usually a false negative self-judgment someone with anxiety gives him or herself. Some people may be just lazy, but most people lack motivation because they feel defeated by the prospect of doing something with anxiety. It feels challenging to even try when anxiety convinces you there's very little chance of success. Anxious people are not unmotivated; they're highly motivated to resist doing what might make them uncomfortable.

Impatience often comes with nervousness or worries. When people are anxious, their mind is filled with the anxious thoughts and feelings giving them less tolerance for anything else.

Overwhelmed is how anxiety makes you feel, because it feels so big and out-of-control. You feel your emotion is more than what you can handle in that moment. It's not pleasant and feeds itself.

Preoccupied is when worries take up the brain space that you could be using for something else.

I use a lot of these terms interchangeably, because I think of them as the same thing. They all have things in common in the way they affect and disempower people.

6. Did I miss one? What name do you give to what you feel? Describe it by writing it down.

_____

_____

_____

7. Cliff Guided Meditation

Do this Cliff Guided Meditation: Read the following and allow yourself 10–20 minutes to envision it.

Get yourself in a relaxed position, lying down or sitting comfortably. Close your eyes and relax into your body, following your breath for a couple of minutes. Once you feel settled and calm, use your imagination to picture yourself on a high cliff of darkness and despair. You may feel afraid and alone here, but also scared to fall off the cliff, thinking it would be the end of you. Imagine your inner wisdom, me, or a best friend there with you. Our guidance comes from love and trust, and we trust you so much more than you do yourself right now. We tell you that it's okay to be vulnerable—that you can handle it. We assure you that you will feel less vulnerable if you leave this cliff and return to life. Take your time to fill yourself with faith and trust. Then, imagine holding our hands and leaping off the cliff together. There's no chaos in our fall. We feel a gentle breeze and softly land into warm, clear water only a few yards off a beautiful bright beach. The darkness and despair are gone and we splash and relax, invigorated by the water and enjoying the natural beauty that surrounds us. We laugh and smile at each other.

Breaking Down
the Power of Anxiety

Here are the six steps I have discovered to curing anxiety, worry, and panic:

1. Understand it Biologically

2. Learn the Lies it Tells

3. Cultivate Your Control

4. Forgive Yourself

5. Repeat Affirmation

6. Practice Daily Rituals

I have mentioned how to learn about the biology of anxiety in my video (jodiaman.com/biology-video/). In Part 2 of this workbook, you are going to expose the lies that anxiety tells, so you can see them coming a mile away and stop believing them!

Perception

Perception is the first way you respond.

Anxiety wants you to see one perspective. Usually the worst case scenario or something equally foreboding. But there are many ways to experience the same event. Did you ever experience something with a friend and are present when he or she tells someone else the story? It is often told slightly different than you remembered. Your friend is not lying. This difference is about perspective, and the way humans remember through the meaning that they create.

Everything that happens to us, every big and little experience, goes through an internal process of meaning making. We assign meanings to everything. We drop an ice cream, that is an annoying accident. We see the bathroom dirty, we are a slob. We see an ambulance go by, someone is hurt. You can see even in my examples that these meanings are just one perspective that reflect my personal past experiences and beliefs.

Here is an alternative perspective: One can drop an ice cream and have the ice cream shop cashier replace it for free and feel happy. One can see a dirty bathroom and worry about a family member being sick the night before. An ambulance going by can remind someone of what she wants to do when she grows up.

If something occurs in life that makes immediate sense, the meaning making process is easy and benign: You start your car and it starts. It's so ordinary, that you barely register it.

But, if what happened is nonsensical (I.e., Someone betrays you.)? This feels out-of-control and scary. The closer you are to a problem, the more chaotic it feels and the harder it is so see more than the negative perspective. The closeness and the chaos limit your view.

8. Practice seeing different perspectives.

This will help you understand there are many ways to look at a situation; some could be negative to you, and others don't have to be. There are no truths in perception, just ideas.

Think about an event you've experienced recently. Write down seven possible explanations for that. Get creative!

Example 1:

Tammy was rude to me last week.

She is preoccupied with a problem.

I caught her off guard.

She was in a hurry and didn't mean to be short with me.

She might have misunderstood something I said.

She was tired or hungry.

She doesn't like me.

I upset her.

Example 2: I didn't get the job I was interviewed for.

The other candidate knew someone.

It wasn't a good fit.

My resume had a typo.

I was only partly what they were looking for.

There was high competition.

I didn't have the right qualifications.

There is something else coming along.

Your turn:

Event_____

1. _____

2. _____

3. _____

4. _____

5. _____

6. _____

Anxiety, worries and fears are constructed by your meaning making and beliefs. You can create anxiety to be very powerful, and if you are here, you probably did.

Oh no, I can't handle this feeling.

Why do I feel this way?

I'm so weak. Nobody else is feeling like this. I can't do this.

I can't because I have anxiety. My mind is wired this way.

I'm vulnerable. How can I live in this world where anything bad can happen?

The future seems miserable.

These are very scary thoughts that make you feel worse. See how there are layers of meaning over each other? To break down these powerful meanings, you need to break down each component of them.

9. Reflect on a worry that you have.

Unpack it by asking it the following questions. (Each question is addressed to the previous answer, so do them in order.)

My worry: _____

What's bad about that?

_____

_____

_____

_____

_____

_____

What is bad about that happening?

_____

_____

_____

_____

_____

And what is bad about that?

_____

_____

_____

_____

Why is that so bad?

_____

_____

_____

_____

What if that happened, how bad would it be?

_____

_____

_____

_____

_____

What is the worst that can happen?

_____

_____

_____

_____

How bad would that be?

_____

_____

_____

_____

Sometimes when you have to go somewhere, anxiety says that you will be really uncomfortable and anxious there and this makes you prefer not to go. It doesn't seem worth the hassle. You'd rather stay where you are comfortable.

Anxiety wants to predict the future and has you assuming failure. It is a con artist. Anxiety creates this meaning out of your fear and it sounds pretty logical and easier, so you believe it. It is actually not easier, it brings suffering. Here is how to build evidence that anxiety is lying when it tells you this stuff.

10. Record assumed vs. actual enjoyment.

Before an event, rate from 1-10 what your anxiety is leading you to believe about how much you will enjoy the event. For example, say I was going to a fundraiser luncheon and I was afraid I would be anxious and trapped there so I just didn't want to go. I would ask myself how much I might enjoy the lunch and probably assume 2 or 3. I would write that down.

Then come hell or high water, I would make myself go. And when I return home, I would rate my actual enjoyment level.

It's usually never as bad as the anxiety says it would be. The higher number would prove that anxiety is lying. Every time you go somewhere, record the before and after. Pretty soon, anxiety's lies won't hold up anymore. Use the next two pages over the next week or so and record the next 10 events.

Add notes and thoughts. It can look like this:

Event: Lunch with friends

Anticipatory anxiety said: 2/10 "It will be awful. You should cancel. Today is not good."

Actual experience: 8/10 It went okay. It was good to laugh with them. Betty was talking about her anxiety. I didn't even know she had it.

Event: Caitlyn's play

Anticipatory anxiety said: 3/10 "There will be so many people. Caitlyn will understand that I can't do it right now."

Actual experience: 9/10! I am so glad I went, Caitlyn did so well. I am so proud of her. She gave me a big hug, what a sweet girl!

Event: _____

Anticipatory anxiety rate: _____

Anticipatory anxiety said: _____

Actual experience rate: _____

Actual experience reflections: _____

_____

Event: _____

Anticipatory anxiety rate: _____

Anticipatory anxiety said: _____

_____

Actual experience rate: _____

Actual experience reflections: _____

_____

Event: _____

Anticipatory anxiety rate: _____

Anticipatory anxiety said: _____

_____

Actual experience rate: _____

Actual experience reflections: _____

_____

Event: _____

Anticipatory anxiety rate: _____

Anticipatory anxiety said: _____

_____

Actual experience rate: _____

Actual experience reflections: _____

_____

Event: _____

Anticipatory anxiety rate: _____

Anticipatory anxiety said: _____

_____

Actual experience rate: _____

Actual experience reflections: _____

_____

Event: _____

Anticipatory anxiety rate: _____

Anticipatory anxiety said: _____

_____

Actual experience rate: _____

Actual experience reflections: _____

_____

Event: _____

Anticipatory anxiety rate: _____

Anticipatory anxiety said: _____

_____

Actual experience rate: _____

Actual experience reflections: _____

_____

Event: _____

Anticipatory anxiety rate: _____

Anticipatory anxiety said: _____

_____

Actual experience rate: _____

Actual experience reflections: _____

_____

Event: _____

Anticipatory anxiety rate: _____

Anticipatory anxiety said: _____

_____

Actual experience rate: _____

Actual experience reflections: _____

_____

Event: _____

Anticipatory anxiety rate: _____

Anticipatory anxiety said: _____

_____

Actual experience rate: _____

Actual experience reflections: _____

_____

I missed so many things when I had anxiety. Things I can't go back to. How often does anxiety have you missing things?

_____

_____

_____

11. **Write some ways** your anxiety has made you believe that it's real and that you should feel scared?

_____

_____

_____

_____

_____

12. **Anxiety affects different aspects of your life.** In the following spaces, write down how anxiety affects these:

Your home:

_____

_____

Your family:

_____

_____

Your school:

_____

_____

Your professional life:

_____

_____

Your social life:

_____

_____

Travel:

_____

_____

Is this okay with you? _____

Why or why not?

_____

_____

_____

_____

When you are exhausted and feel like giving up the effort of getting rid of anxiety, you need to go back to your initial motivation.

Sayonara

13. Write a goodbye note to "Anxiety."

Example:

Dear (or Not So Dear) Fear and Anxiety,

You are both the same to me, as is Guilt! You have run my life for way too long and I have had enough! I will no longer allow you to set my path in life. You have taken me down into the bowels of Hell and I refuse to live there any longer. You have made me feel worthless, incapable, stupid, and unlovable, and I will not tolerate it. You have taken my self-esteem and squashed it. You have made me believe that it is all my fault and I don't deserve anything better. But, I have discovered that you are a liar! Everything you put into my head is a lie.

Sometimes you whisper and sometimes you scream, but they are all lies about me and my place in this universe. I cannot and will not have a relationship with a liar, someone who sucks the very life out of me! I have been a coward in your presence. I have let you do with me what you wish. You have hurt me thousands of times and I still allowed you in my life. You have kept me down, telling me not to try anything new because I will fail. Telling me it's too late for me to grow, but grow I will! Telling me I am incapable of love! Incapable of handling challenging experiences! Telling me I cannot heal or heal others! Telling me that I am nothing without you! Well, no more! I am everything without you!

Since I've discovered exactly what you are, I no longer want you in my life! So go away! Forever!

If you insist on returning, each and every time I will send you packing! You cannot be a part of my life anymore. You have done nothing but hurt me over and over again. I will not accept that from anyone, least of all you! No matter what you say, no matter how deep inside me you get, I know that I am a worthy, capable and lovable person. And I know that as long as I keep sending you away, the less power you will have over me, until you wither away to the nothingness that you really are!

I refuse to believe your accusations or tolerate your disrespect! It's done! No matter what you do, it's done. You are no longer welcome in my life!

With all the strength of Truth and Love on my side,

James

It's your turn. Write your goodbye letter to anxiety

Dear Anxiety,

_____

_____

_____

_____

_____

_____

_____

_____

_____

_____

_____

_____

_____

_____

_____

14. Decrease your fear of fear.

1. Talk about your anxiety

a. Say your worries aloud to an empty room. Listen to yourself. Do they sound as bad as they are in your head? Repeat them over and over until your nervous energy decreases. You can even repeat, "I'm so scared. I'm so scared. I'm so scared. I'm so scared..." Imagine you are letting air out of a big balloon until it's very small and weak.

b. Find a friend you can text out your fears to when they come up. This should be someone you trust and who doesn't judge you. Anytime you feel a worry or fear, type it out and send it to them. Allow them to dissuade your fears and help you laugh it off.

2. Have planned "Worry time"

Organize a call with a good friend to catch up, have your favorite movie cued up, or set up an activity that brings you joy and comfort.

Just before you do that, try Planned Worry Time. Set a timer for a few minutes. Give yourself permission to let all your worries flow as intense and as big as they feel. Write them down, draw them, speak them, or do whatever helps you getting them from inside of you to the outside. Don't judge them. If they stop, keep asking more to come.

When the timer goes off, thank your worries graciously for coming out. Close the session with some empowering, encouraging words to yourself like, "I did it! I'm awesome!" Do a victory dance and head right into the activity you've set up.

3. Identify some times when you were forced to face your fears due to circumstances beyond your control (having to conquer your fear of heights to rescue your cat).

_____

_____

_____

_____

Negative Self-Judgment

Anxiety and negative self-judgment go hand-in-hand. The more you judge yourself harshly the more susceptible you are to anxiety. If you think you are inadequate and not good enough, you won't trust yourself. Trust is the opposite of anxiety. The biggest lie that anxiety says is that you can't handle things. If you trusted yourself to handle anything, especially the anxiety, it wouldn't come.

The more you beat yourself up about your inadequacies, the more you will feel vulnerable, the more anxiety can take you over. To solve the anxiety, you need to be kinder to yourself. Negative self-judgments are sneaky, which makes it hard to see them as self-judgments. It is time to bring them out into the open where you can see them for what they are.

If you don't notice any negative self-judgments right away, that doesn't mean that they are not there. Even if you don't notice they still can bring you down. Ask yourself to bring your awareness to them in the next couple of days. You may start to notice when you are being hard on yourself without even realizing it. Come back to this page and jot it down. This practice in noticing them will help you discredit them.

15. What negative self-judgments have anxiety been trying to get you to believe?

_____

_____

_____

_____

_____

_____

_____

16. How does your anxiety disguise itself?

_____

_____

_____

_____

_____

17. Write down your worst fears.

Next to each one put a number between 1 and 10 representing how likely it is to happen, with 10 being "It's absolutely likely." Then, decide how much time and energy it's worth on a scale of 1-10, 10 being worth all of your time.

Worst fear	Likelihood 1–10	Worth it? 1–10
_____	_____	_____
_____	_____	_____
_____	_____	_____
_____	_____	_____
_____	_____	_____
_____	_____	_____
_____	_____	_____
_____	_____	_____

I hope this part of the book has exposed anxiety for what it is: A dirty rotten liar. Now you will be more able to distinguish your voice from anxiety's.

18. Practice what you learned so far about the lies anxiety tells.

Below is a list of thoughts that you might have. Some are examples of the anxiety talking, and some are examples of your wisdom. See if you can notice the difference. Circle the thoughts that are your wisdom. Put a line through anxiety's lies.

I can't do this.

I always get hurt in relationships.

I'm different from everyone else.

Oh, no, I might panic right now.

I'll just get out of bed. I may feel better.

I can't eat.

I should take a walk.

Breathe.

This is not going to work.

I can't go. Something bad will happen.

I can't handle this. It's not worth even trying.

There's Sally. I can stand near her.

Oh, no, I'm going to panic! I have to get out of here.

I'll call Cindy. She'll help me feel better.

I won't worry about getting it all done. I'll just begin.

It's going to be okay.

I'm not okay!

I'm weak.

I'm alone.

I'm not alone, and I've done it before!

Now it's your turn—write the phrases anxiety uses on you.

_____

_____

_____

_____

_____

_____

_____

_____

_____

_____

_____

_____

_____

Write down some of the confident things you say to debunk anxiety and help calm yourself down.

_____

_____

_____

_____

_____

_____

_____

_____

_____

_____

_____

_____

_____

Cultivate Your Control

Control issues are anxiety issues. Being out of control entices fear, and you have to learn how to build trust in yourself and your skills, so you feel in control.

Mostly you are told by experts that you have to surrender control to be happy. This didn't work for me when I was too anxious white knuckling my grip on what I didn't want to lose control of. I became defensive and held tighter.

There are many things in life that you can feel out of control about (other people, accidents, weather, and health). When you focus on what you are out of control about life can be very scary. What helped me the most is to see that I have 100% of control over what matters. I have 100% of control over my response.

Why does response matter most? Because your response is how you think about an event, how you give meaning to it, what you do next, how you treat people, and how compassionate you are to yourself. This affects your overall health, your emotions, your relationships, your mental state and spiritual journey. Your response (of which you have 100% of control) regulates your overall happiness or sadness in life.

This idea is what helped me relax that grip. The only thing I had to attach to was trust in myself, and then, I didn't have to worry about being out of control again.

Anxiety mostly makes you NOT trust yourself, so building this trust (confidence and belief in yourself) is a job we have to do for you. In this next part of the workbook, we are going to focus on your skills and abilities so that you can feel more in control than you have felt in a long time.

Before we start cultivating your control, remind yourself:

19. What is more important to you than satisfying the anxiety?

_____

_____

_____

_____

_____

_____

_____

_____

20. Write down what is important to you about yourself, your abilities, your family or your career.

_____

_____

_____

_____

_____

_____

_____

Read it over and over. Do this when you're calm. Then when the anxiety comes, it's at the forefront of your mind and harder to forget.

21. Watch my webinar training: *15 Lies That Anxiety Tells* jodiaman.com/webinar

Do the practice mentioned in this video. Every morning write five achievable goals for yourself on a post it.

1. Mow lawn

2. Call the dentist

3. Email the teacher

4. Complete and send in form

5. Work out

Cross them out when you are done so you can take that moment to celebrate it.

Every night before you go to bed, write down three things that you accomplished during the day. (They can be your goals or something else.)

1. Planted the vegetables.

2. Washed all the towels.

3. Finished a blog post.

This is like a gratitude journal but different since you are recording something that you do, instead of something you can just passively observe. I want you to see daily reminders of your skills and abilities that are always there, but that you probably don't celebrate. We humans are constantly looking at what we still have to do, what we messed up and what we are failing to do. This practice will bring your attention to the millions of things you do every day, but don't acknowledge. Once you start to notice them, you will build your self-confidence.

Gratitude journals are awesome too and life-changing. Please add writing down three things that you are grateful for each day to this exercise, since it takes but a minute and has lasting benefits.

Here is space for the next ten days to get you started. Thereafter, continue in your own journal. Try this practice for at least two months, until you notice that you started to celebrate your accomplishments all through the day, feel more confident, and are happier in general. As you get better at noticing, your list can run longer than three!

Date: _____

Three things I did today:

_____

_____

_____

Skills used: _____

Three things I am grateful for:

_____

_____

_____

Date: _____

Three things I did today:

_____

_____

_____

Skills used: _____

Three things I am grateful for:

_____

_____

_____

Date: _____

Three things I did today:

_____

_____

_____

Skills used: _____

Three things I am grateful for:

_____

_____

_____

Date: _____

Three things I did today:

_____

_____

_____

Skills used: _____

Three things I am grateful for:

_____

_____

_____

Date: _____

Three things I did today:

_____

_____

_____

Skills used: _____

Three things I am grateful for:

_____

_____

_____

Date: _____

Three things I did today:

_____

_____

_____

Skills used: _____

Three things I am grateful for:

_____

_____

_____

Date: _____

Three things I did today:

_____

_____

_____

Skills used: _____

Three things I am grateful for:

_____

_____

_____

Date: _____

Three things I did today:

_____

_____

_____

Skills used: _____

Three things I am grateful for:

_____

_____

_____

Date: _____

Three things I did today:

_____

_____

_____

Skills used: _____

Three things I am grateful for:

_____

_____

_____

Date: _____

Three things I did today:

_____

_____

_____

Skills used: _____

Three things I am grateful for:

_____

_____

_____

22. Reflect on your decisions.

Have decisions been hard for you to make? Do you tend to worry that you can't trust yourself?

Write a list of some good decisions you've made in your life. Big and small.

Then, add what these actions/decisions say about you as a person.

Example: I started the dinner in the Crock-Pot in the morning. I'm responsible and organized.

1. _____

2. _____

3. _____

4. _____

5. _____

6. _____

7. _____

We are always getting ready to live and never living. ~Ralph Waldo Emerson

Are you ready?

What do you do when you are not ready? There are way too many things that get in the way of doing what we want to do, and doing what we feel like we are meant to do in this life.

These things have us dragging our feet, making excuses, waiting for the perfect time, and letting opportunities pass us by.

I'm not talking about procrastinating chores that you don't want to do. I'm talking about doing things that you WANT to do. Your dream. Your life mission. Relationships. Your purpose.

Why does this happen? You can have tons of reasons (or excuses) to wait, but fear is often behind the big ones. What fears you have about getting started?

Maybe...

It might not work out.

I may not be able to do it.

It might be a mistake.

What if I mess up.

I don't trust anyone.

It may be too hard.

It will take too much time.

It may take me away from people that I love.

If I succeed, will it change me?

It's great to be very clear on what this fear is, because when it is evasive, it has more power. Say it out loud. Write it down. Know it well. That's how you begin to get the power back.

23. What are your reasons for waiting?

_____

_____

_____

_____

_____

24. List times in your life where you waited to be ready before taking action, but that time never came (a high school crush you wanted to talk to, but graduation came and went before you worked up the courage to take that step).

_____

_____

_____

_____

_____

_____

Next time, start before you are ready. Just start with something easy and just take one little step.

Starting is the hardest part, and when you convince yourself it is just one tiny step, it makes it easier to begin.

This first step will usually give you enough encouragement, energy, and confidence for the next small step.

Remember: that step doesn't have to be perfect. It is more important to make it happen, than it is to make it perfect.

Perfection doesn't exist. You can kill yourself trying to achieve it. It will always come in between you and happiness. Striving for perfection will erode your soul and zap you of your power.

Let it go and take that step!

Little steps aren't insignificant. You add them up and magic can happen.

Have compassion for yourself through the process. Give yourself loads of kudos. This acknowledgment serves you with energy! Celebrate small successes.

LEARN MORE ABOUT YOUR VULNERABILITY AND YOUR POWER. START MY FREE VIDEO SERIES: THEMAPTOWHOLEPEACE.COM

25. Take a walk outside today.

Sometimes you have to work on getting rid of anxiety, but too much anxiety talk can just bring it on, because you are still giving it your attention. Make sure you take some breaks in the process where you don't think about it. Taking walks is wonderful because walking burns off nervous energy. Walking benefits you in four ways.

Physically you release endorphins, GABA and tryptophan that calm you down.

---

4 Watch my video on *5 Ways Nature Helps* with Anxiety on YouTube.

Mentally you have other things—the world around you, people, and nature—to focus on. **Emotionally** you are building confidence in yourself because you did something good for you. **Spiritually** you feel more empowered and connected to the world.[4]

If it's cold out, bundle up. The exercise will warm you from within. Check your level of anxiety 1–10 before you leave and then again after you are finished. Did your anxiety go down at all?

26. Relax.

While distracting yourself by doing something is great to ward off anxiety, you also want to include in your repertoire activities that slow you down. Everyone needs rest.

Don't look at these activities as risky—having a blank mind vulnerable to anxiety. See them as giving your brain something easy and relaxing to focus on to help your body recover from constant stress.

There are relaxing activities that increase your GABA. (GABA is the hormone that puts the brakes on the stress hormones.) Get something small to focus on like a candle flame, music or the sounds of nature. Take a shower, soak in a tub, give yourself a massage and get some rest.

Once you feel more calm and clearer, find something creative and enjoyable to take your attention.

Make a list of relaxing, but mind occupying activities that you can have in your tool box.

1. _____

2. _____

3. _____

4. _____

5. _____

6. _____

Planning

Planning is an excellent skill. Plans give you something to feel secure about. You need to make sure that the plan is not rigid so that you won't go off the rails if something goes wrong. Plans that are flexible and include what-ifs and escape-plans are the best. Plans ought to have you explore your problems solving skills not your control skills.

27. Make a plan.

Think of an activity coming up soon.

What might possibly change? What can you do about it?

_____

_____

_____

_____

_____

See From the Big Picture

Most of the time, we are so close to the chaos of our problems, that we see the small slice of our immediate world. If that is going downhill and your suffering is increasing, only seeing that small slice can be overwhelming. If you had the distance to see your life from a big picture you can see that despite the downs, there are some ups too. Seeing this way can give you faith that you'll get through it just like you always have and life will turn around again soon.

28. Check out this diagram of the ups and downs of life. The circled area in the beginning of July indicates that this person is going through a difficult period.

When you are inside the circle what do you see and experience?

_____

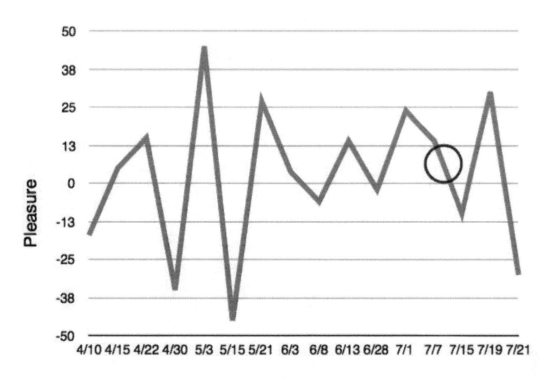

Time

_____

_____

_____

_____

What do you notice when you see the whole chart from the big picture view?

_____

_____

_____

_____

When you look from the big picture you can see anxiety as an experience. You see that despite how horrible it has been, you have learned from it. Maybe you learned to ask for what you need, you learned to prioritize self care, or set limits with negative people.

29. Write down five things you have learned from anxiety.

1. _____

2. _____

3. _____

4. _____

5. _____

30. Reflect on your present situation and think about times in the past where you have felt a similar panic.

List them here.

_____

_____

_____

_____

_____

Now think back to how you came through these situations. Make a list of actions you took to survive them.

_____

_____

_____

_____

_____

31. Demand answers from "Anxiety" to the following questions.

You answer as if you are in the head of personified anxiety. What would Anxiety say...

What do you want from me?

_____

_____

Why do you want to ruin my life?

_____

_____

Why do you tell me that you're more powerful than me?

_____

_____

Why do you make me feel like I'll have to deal with you forever?

_____

_____

Why do you make me doubt the things I know to be true (i.e., I've done it before.)?

_____

_____

Why do you make me feel powerless?

_____

_____

Why do you sometimes come out of the blue?

_____

_____

Why do you have me thinking that I'm weak?

_____

_____

Why do you try to separate me from all those who love me?

_____

_____

How do you convince me to listen to you?

_____

_____

Why do you have me focus on the worst possible scenario?

_____

_____

Why do you lie to me?

_____

_____

Why do I believe you?

_____

_____

What would my life be like, if I didn't let you in?

_____

_____

Why don't you just leave me alone?

_____

_____

32. Now, ask yourself these questions.

Why do you believe Anxiety is more powerful than you are?

_____

What has made you feel powerless?

_____

_____

What skills have you used to get through hard times in the past?

_____

_____

What is your biggest motivator to get rid of anxiety?

_____

_____

Why is that important?

_____

_____

What do you want to tell Anxiety?

_____

_____

When do you want to reclaim your life from anxiety?

_____

_____

What skills have you used in getting over anxiety in the past?

_____

_____

How do you know you can do this?

_____

_____

_____

Who is around that believes in you?

_____

_____

_____

33. Remember.

Pick one or more person who know and care about you from your past or present. You can connect with them by thinking of how they influenced you, even if they're not with you physically. List them here.

_____

_____

_____

_____

Think about them and ask yourself:

What does he/she appreciate about me?

_____

_____

_____

_____

How did he/she contribute to who I am today?

_____

_____

_____

_____

How did I contribute to his/her life?

_____

_____

_____

_____

_____

Anxiety wants all of your attention. But life is too precious. You have other things that you would like to give your energy to, things that you LOVE so much more and would be so much more worth your time.

34. Make a list of people, things or issues that are important to you.

_____

_____

_____

_____

_____

35. Looking at your list above, who/what inspires/motivates you to face your fears?

How can you use this to push through your fears?

_____

_____

_____

_____

36. Commit to making an effort to heal by writing down what you want to do, if fear didn't stop you.

Here are some examples.

Today, I will exercise without letting fear stop me.

Today, I will speak up to my co-worker without letting fear stop me.

This week, I will tell Josie how I feel without letting fear stop me.

This month, I will clean out the closet without letting fear stop me.

Today, I will _____

_____

This week, I will _____

_____

This month, I will _____

_____

This year, I will _____

_____

37. This is why my fears are unnecessary...

_____

_____

_____

_____

38. It is helpful to know the first small step, so you don't get overwhelmed doing your above goals for today, this week, etc. Rather than write down the huge goal, write down the first small step to achieving it.

This is the first step to doing what I want today:

_____

_____

_____

_____

_____

When you personify anxiety, it not only helps you separate it from your identity, but it helps you understand it better. Plus you become an outside observer which is a place from which you can validate yourself!

39. Draw your fear.

40. Now make it silly.

Write a funny poem about it. Draw it in a ridiculous way. Tell a goofy story to take the power right out of it.

"The two most important days in your life are the day you were born and the day you find out why." ~Mark Twain

Five Rules to a Happy Life

I want this for you because a happy life is a much easier way for you to live on this planet. I am your greatest fan and I want you to be relieved of this suffering.

However, you being happy is also important beyond your own pleasure. How you are in the world affects you, but it also affects everyone around you, including the plants and the animals. When you switch your fear energy to trust energy, you are changing negative energy in the world to positive energy.

Think of The Butterfly Effect. A small change as minor as the flap of a butterfly's wing can provoke a bigger variation at a different time and place, like a hurricane. Isn't it nice to know that if you felt better, it might have an even larger positive impact?

The pain in the world, the greed, the selfishness and the getting power over other people, all come from feeling unhappy. So when you heal yourself, and live your life to the fullest in your highest possible destiny way, you also lift up and improve the lives of those around you, changing the world into a better place to be.

Here are my five rules to life:

1. Make people important

    a. Be present and have compassion

    b. Choose people over tasks

    c. Don't jump to solving people's problems. Only give advice if you are asked three times, as unsolicited advice makes a person feel judged.

    d. Remember people are fragile.

    e. Be kind to yourself—you are a person! (See blog: jodiaman.com/embrace-yourself/)

2. Step back

Whatever you feel, give yourself compassion. (Say, "I get it.") Practice stepping back from the chaos of any situation that distresses you. Gain a big picture perspective. Give it a bit of time. Ask for spiritual guidance if you have faith. And then decide what to do.

"People are not mean because they don't like you, they are mean because they don't like themselves." ~Jodi Aman

3. Have fun

The three steps to happiness:

   a. Let go what you don't want,

   b. Bring in what you do want, and

   c. Practice every day.

Happiness is not what lucky people have. It is generated by practicing—by creating a vision for who you want to be in the world and taking action every day to step into that.[5]

Problems like anxiety, depression, and worthlessness can be very serious dudes. When we lighten up about them and ourselves, life gets so much easier. Create opportunities to laugh by watching comedy. Bring joy to everything, even annoying chores.

4. Be creative

You need a creative pursuit in your life. Mentally, it improves the function and health of the prefrontal cortex decreasing anxiety and depression. Emotionally, it builds confidence and self-trust. Spiritually, it gives a sense of purpose and contribution. Relationally, it gets you closer to people. Physically, it keeps you moving.

One of the most depressing things for people is when they lack a purpose. They feel untethered. They have no sense of self. They feel quite lost and it doesn't feel good to their soul.

5. Practice doing hard things

The most important thing to your happiness is having faith in yourself. To know that whatever comes your way, you can figure it out. You must build up this trust by practicing doing hard things.

---

5 See blog: jodiaman.com/secrets-of-happy-people/

Writing down goals for the day give you a 9x more chances at doing what you wrote.

"If it is important to you, you will find a way. If not, you'll find an excuse."   ~Unknown

41. Commit to one nourishing practice right now.

I am going to add this to my morning routine...

_____

_____

_____

_____

_____

_____

How To Love Yourself When You Don't Like Yourself Too Much

Did you ever wonder how to love yourself when you don't like yourself very much? We've got all these opinions about ourselves. We're not good enough, we're not smart enough, we're too fat, we're stupid, we've made problems in the past, we've messed things up, and we don't like ourselves very much.

We compare ourselves to everyone else around us and they all seem great while we're in trouble or in a problem or suffering in some way. This makes us think that we don't love ourselves. I think this negative self-judgment might indicate you're not liking yourself and is totally different than *loving yourself.*

The problem is that we don't really know what loving ourselves means.

For me, it means just being in the present moment with myself—just being okay in the present moment. It means not having judgments, *at all.* It is when we're absolutely in the present moment and just breathing and saying as an observer, "Okay, this is me here breathing." It is THAT simple.

I know you have some self-love since you expressed your worth at some time or another. At some point you have defended yourself, "It's not fair that this happened" or "I wouldn't choose to feel this way," "People who are depressed don't choose to feel depressed." You have done this before, right? Everybody has done this.

For me, this defense says that a part of you believes you are worthy and do not deserve feeling this way. If you feel that sense of worth at some point even if it is somewhere deep inside, you do have self-love. Whether you realize it or not, whether you also think of yourself as unworthy (because humans can have contradictory beliefs), it is there.

The problem is that often people think that they have to like themselves in order to love themselves and that the negative self-judgments are too high to do that.

When you think that you don't have self-love, then you can't access it or feel it. When you hear a speaker or author direct you to "feel self-love in your heart" you might be like "Oh my gosh! I don't feel anything. Maybe I don't feel love. I guess I don't know how to love. I don't know how to love myself. I don't love myself." You totally freak out.

Self-love is very abstract. It is not something tangible that you feel. There is actually nothing to feel. It's just breath and the present moment. That's it. You have it.

42. Have self-compassion.

Write out some feelings you have about something that happened recently. Beside each feeling write "...and I understand why I feel that way," or "...and it's okay that I feel that way." (This is so simple, you might worry you don't understand the exercise. See my examples.) Read what you write aloud to yourself.

Examples:

I'm hurt when nobody helps me... and I understand why I feel that way.

I was angry that she blew me off... and it's okay to feel that way.

1. _____

2. _____

3. _____

4. _____

5. _____

6. _____

7. _____

43. List out your skills and knowledges.

During hard or tricky times, what got you through? What did you do in the past when you had/felt anxiety? What are some things that you appreciate about yourself?

If this is hard to answer, look at yourself through someone else's eyes. What do they appreciate about you?

_____

_____

_____

_____

_____

44. Feel your feelings meditation.

One of my absolute favorites...

Find yourself a quiet space to sit and close your eyes. Think about a feeling, the raw feeling, not the story—not judgment, blame, regret—just the feeling. For this short period of time you are going to suspend the story about it. Imagine that feeling in your body somewhere and see it as if it is a shape, image or color. (Like a thick black cloud over your heart, or a rock in your stomach.) Pretend you are sitting in a folding chair watching yourself with this feeling-shape in you. You are witnessing this shape in your body and feeling the feeling, without the story. You see and feel the shape, but you don't know what it means. (If the story comes back in your mind, that's okay. Gently and compassionately let it go and go back to experiencing the raw feeling.)

Now, breathe into that shape. Take five long, slow breaths. Then, check in with yourself and notice if anything has changed. Don't assess, just notice. Then, repeat the process: five long breaths and stop to notice. Continue this until the shape changes, becomes benign, transformed, or is completely dissolved. This may take three to thirty minutes.[6]

45. Affirmations that work.

Current belief: I can't get better.

Desired belief: I will get better.

Create the first affirmation describing something you can believe, even if just to a certain extent.

First affirmation: There may be, however small and remote, a possibility that I can get better even though I don't see it right now.

Say this first affirmation twelve times, three times a day. Program it into your phone as a reminder. Discipline yourself not to shortcut this process. This is an effort, but it's the easiest thing you'll do all day. Don't dismiss it because it's too easy. It works!

Repeat this until you believe it fully. Then write another one.

Second affirmation: There might be a possibility that I can get better.

Say that one twelve times, three times a day for as many days, weeks or months as you need to feel it and believe it all the way into your heart. Just keep it up until you believe it absolutely and fully.

---

6 Find my free audio version of this online: jodiaman.com/you1anxiety0

Remember, don't get distressed about how much time it takes. That just invites judgment. The more compassion and the less judgment you have, the better.

Write the next affirmation.

Third affirmation: I may be better. I think I can get better.

Say that as long as you need to. Then make a slight shift.

Fourth affirmation: I am getting better. Or, it doesn't have to be scary to heal.

Here is another example:

Current belief: I am not forgivable.

Desired belief: I am forgivable.

First affirmation: It may be possible that I can forgive myself for this.

Once the first affirmation is accepted and believed, you can take the affirmation one step further.

Second affirmation: It's possible that I can forgive myself for this.

Be gentle with yourself. Have compassion even for the process of deciding to have compassion!

Once you have this, move on to the next affirmation.

Third affirmation: I deserve forgiveness for this.

Fourth affirmation: I can forgive myself. And so on.

These are just examples to help you see the process. Your affirmations will be tailored to what fits for you. Each next affirmation will depend on what is going on for you in the moment. Keep making affirmations that get you gradually closer to the place you would like to be. Take small steps, as small as you need, then bigger when you're ready. There is no finite number of steps that you are going for.

Affirmations are easy. It's so simple to make big, lasting changes to your heart and mind. I'm excited for you to feel the peace and serenity they bring.

It's time to let go. You know it is—that's why you're here. Just give yourself a hug for being here. Remember, compassion is the key. You deserve it to be free.

46. Let go.

Ask yourself:

What do I want to move past?

_____

_____

_____

_____

What do I want to let go?

_____

_____

_____

_____

What negative thing do I think about myself?

_____

_____

_____

_____

47. Create affirmations.

What are the desired beliefs?

_____

_____

_____

_____

_____

_____

Here are some stepping-stone affirmations.

_____

_____

_____

_____

_____

_____

48. Record your worries and anxieties over the next two weeks.

Worry	How bad is it?	Action	Next day, How did I do?
_____	_____	_____	_____
_____	_____	_____	_____
_____	_____	_____	_____
_____	_____	_____	_____
_____	_____	_____	_____
_____	_____	_____	_____
_____	_____	_____	_____
_____	_____	_____	_____

49. Breathe.

Practice this favorite breathing technique for panic:

Inhale for the count of five.

Hold for count of five.

Exhale for count of five.

Take two regular breaths.

If you are having trouble breathing it is probably because your lungs are full. When you hyperventilate, you keep trying to inhale, and it doesn't work because your lungs are full. That's why the ole' paper bag works. It reminds you to exhale.

I dedicate this note to those of you who are holding your breath. You know who you are. The ones waiting for relief, needing some good news, longing for "this" to pass, or wishing for a hug saying it is all going to be okay. Sometimes we don't even know we are holding our breath, holding our shoulders up, holding up our lives—worried, stressed... preoccupied. ON hold.

Listen. Exhale. I finally did today and I want to pass it around. It's not over, it is never over, but it's not all losses. Sometimes there are wins. Things change. People figure it out, time goes on. The light comes again every morning after darkness. There is always hope. It is not over. Everything changes. If you are going through hell, keep going. Believe in the good of people around you. Believe in your ability to turn things around to what you'd prefer. Hold that vision, that purpose and make choices in that direction. Even if you get it wrong sometimes or make a mistake—embrace your humanness and keep trying.

It is all just stories. The story is not over. It continues to change. Breathe through the story.

You can go through it holding your breath or go through it breathing. Holding your breath doesn't help. You still go through it!

But... you come out easier if you have breathed and trusted Spirit, yourself and your friends. It's still hell, but going through hell with hope is infinitely better.

Breathe, loves. It gets better. Be easy on yourself. Have compassion. Listen to your guides. They are always with you. You are never alone. Rest knowing all the responsibility of the world is NOT on your shoulders. Breathe. Stay in the present moment. Repeat after me. "This too shall pass."

I've seen it pass too many times for so many people, to not trust it.

You can persevere. And you don't have to do it alone.

If you are struggling and would like some personalized help, I do that, too. You can work with me in a group or individually.

50. Celebrate YOU.

Make a poster displaying a list of your skills, knowledges and accomplishments. If you have trouble, ask a loved one for help. Refer back to this list often. Decorate it, make it your own, and post it somewhere prominent. Take a photo of it on your phone, so you can refer to it anytime.

Read your list twelve times in the morning, twelve times at noon, and twelve times at night. Counting gives it a structure to help your brain take it in. Twelve gives you a goal. It's not so many it becomes tedious, but enough to have it stick.

Remember, it's very important to read through your list when you're feeling calm. I can't stress this enough. Don't wait until you're anxious before pulling out this list. You can use it when you're anxious, but only after you've practiced for at least several days when you're calm.

Dear Love,

I hope you enjoyed this workbook and will keep practicing. It is not an exhaustive account on how to help with anxiety like my paperback *You 1, Anxiety 0*. It is meant as a companion to that, another tool to help you change your thinking through practice.

Smile often. Hug and touch people often. Open your heart. Keep hoping. You are so amazing and worthy for doing what you do. Now let's have it work in your favor!

Remember there is no "I" in T-E-A-M. Anxiety wants you isolated, so you do the opposite. If you want a safe community to talk with others like you, join mine online.

jodiaman.com

facebook.com/jodiamanlove

Instagram @jodiamanlove

YouTube Jodi Aman

Twitter @JodiAman

Pinterest JodiAman

Little birds, thank you so much for giving your recovery your time and attention. You deserve to be happy and free. Go out there and let that you, that you want to be, shine through.

Big Hugs,

Jodi
xoxo

About the Author

Jodi Aman knows people. She is a practicing psychotherapist who has worked with 35 people a week for 20 years in Rochester, NY. She got her Master's in Science in Social Work from Columbia University in 1996 and has studied and taught Narrative Therapy around the world focusing on trauma and anxiety recovery.

Jodi films and edits her own YouTube channel and has five online courses with a focus on getting rid of anxiety and empowering people to have more joy in their lives. She plays herself in *The Secrets of the Keys* self-help movie.

Jodi knows anxiety. In her youth she was immobilized by her own panic and anxiety, yet she clawed her way back to life, and taught herself to master happiness. In this bestselling book *You 1, Anxiety 0,* she shows readers how to win their life back from fear and panic, helping them find peace in their days.

As an inspirational speaker, she helps audiences make sense of their lives. She shows how to shift thinking, change unwanted situations, and finally stop the out-of-control downward spiral by releasing that internal self-critic.

Do you want to go deeper with Jodi?

Find out how to work with with her at jodiaman.com

Click "Work with me" at the top!

Anxiety-Free Me!

5 week comprehensive online anxiety recovery program!

- Group coaching so it is personalized to YOU.

- Connect with a community that lifts you up and understands.

- Learn what anxiety is and why it is so powerful.

- Get practical tips on how to take it down.

- Change the triggers in your brain.

- Find your life purpose. Find yourself.

- Improve your relationships.

- Live happy and at peace.

- 40+ videos, audios and handouts - for life.

Get it here: https://jodiaman.com/anxiety-training

Anxiety-Free Kids!

Online anxiety recovery
for parents and kids!

- Immediate access to over 20 videos, audios and fun handouts for you and your child, for life.

- Find out exactly what to do when you can't stand to see your child suffer anymore!

- Kid-friendly videos featuring my baby girl, Miss Lily Aman!

- Hear directly from the horse's mouth as I interview Anxiety herself!

- Access to a private FB group and get support from people who know what you are going through.

- Have fun and feel freedom from anxiety!

Get it here: https://jodiaman.com/anxiety-training

Driving Anxiety Help

Drive relaxed and in control!

- Feel in control when you drive.
- Drive your family to places where you'd get to spend quality time and create memories.
- Don't miss another party - no matter which part of town it's in!
- Go to that concert or convention with your friends.
- Get to work without the stress.
- Six downloadable mp3s to listen to while you are driving.
- Build a sturdy self-confidence.

Get it here: https://jodiaman.com/anxiety-training

Flying Free From Fear

Get rid of flying anxiety with this meditation series.

- Three mp3s to prepare you for your flight.

- Eight more to use while you are flying.

- Start your recovery as soon as you book your trip.

- Feel in control before you fly.

- Put your family first and your fear last.

- Don't miss or avoid another adventure.

- Have more fun in your life.

- See those ancient ruins!

- Fly to whatever you want.

Get it here: https://jodiaman.com/anxiety-training